GOD NEEL

WHY CHRISTIAN BELIEFS FAIL

GW00857361

J. D. BRUCKER

For Those Willing To Question

"It is a horrible idea that there is somebody who owns us, who makes us, who supervises us, waking and sleeping, who knows our thoughts, who can convict us of thought crime, who can—thought crime, just for what we think, who can judge us while we sleep for things that might occur to us in our dreams, who can create us sick, as apparently we are, and then order us on pain of eternal torture to be well again. To demand this, to wish this to be true it to wish to live as an abject slave. It is a wonderful thing, it is a wonderful thing, in my submission, that we now have enough information, enough intelligence, and I hope, enough intellectual and moral courage to say that this ghastly proposition is founded on a lie and to celebrate that fact and I invite you to join me in doing so."

Christopher Hitchens

CONTENTS

NOTE FROM THE AUTHOR

This book serves as a second, revised edition of God Needs To Go (self-published in 2012). This book is now published by Atheist Republic. Thank you for your support.

II

YOU AREN'T ALONE

Some atheists know how it is to live as if they're someone else. The most fortunate are the atheists who grow up in a society, or family structure, that maintains an open sense of secularism. As a former Christian living in the United States, I understand how it feels to pretend in front of those I care about. Since I've come out as an outspoken atheist, many things have changed; I've lost friends and family, but what's truly important is what I've gained. I've gained an even bigger family, one that does not hold prejudice or anger towards simply thinking differently.

Atheist Republic is the quintessential resource for those looking to find a voice they never believed they possessed. Since I began writing for the organization, I've seen firsthand the lives we've touched, the minds we've changed, and the comfort we've given. We are here for you when you're feeling lost. With a massive community in almost every social media network, there will never be a moment you're too far from support. We at Atheist Republic have built a community worthy of respect. Here, you will always be someone important. If you are an atheist, afraid to face an uncertain future, just remember this statement: You are not alone.

INTRODUCTION

"Faith is believing something you know ain't true." - Mark Twain, *Following the Equator*

Beginning in the early first century of the Common Era, an enticing and incredible presumption has been maintained by the greater majority of theistic adherents. It is the belief in the formal existence of the spiritual Jesus Christ and his everlasting father. From birth, individuals are told that their existence on Earth bares a single purpose; to follow an invisible being with the utmost respect and gratitude. His love and acceptance gives them strength and comfort at a level they believe to be unobtainable by others. He silently watches over them from an invisible perch, guiding metaphysically through their own actions and influencing them by presenting daunting situations that test their abilities as an individual. A life in the name of Jesus will eventually culminate in heaven where the essence of God will surround them. There is only one problem with this assertion: It simply isn't true.

Christianity can systematically destroy any sense of rational thinking that an individual may possess. A Christian's level of understanding has been thwarted by the injection of those unfounded claims, which is rooted in tribal beliefs. When presented with evidence to the contrary, their initial response is to cast reason aside and proclaim that faith will always surpass anything that science can prove. It is up to the believer what type of reasonable understandings they will allow to circumvent his or her belief in an omnipotent and omnipresent God. The passageway for such a detachment within the individual will, and will always, remain narrow so much so that a level of intellectualism will forever be unobtainable. They will continue with these beliefs with the utmost conviction until they allow themselves to think freely.

Science and reason have inadvertently done a sufficient job of removing the necessity to believe that all matter, living and intimate, are a created product of an all-knowing being. History has painted a vivid tale of deception, greed, anger, hate mongering, death, torture, bigotry, misogyny, war, racism, and stupidity, all originating from a central point: Christianity. Thousands upon thousands have been killed in the name of God, and millions have had the true nature of our wonderful universe struck away from them by their reserved outlook. At their core, they are as atheistic as I, but as you slowly rise to the surface and explore every facet of their faith, it demonstrates the power of what one single idea can invoke inside the mind of the believer.

This belief was founded on invalid assumptions made by those who were unable to obtain the knowledge needed to understand the world in which they dwelled. Life was as mysterious as it was complicated, and an answer for those troubling questions is something we strive for even today. We want to believe we have a purpose on Earth; that our limited time on this planet is meant to be something more fruitful than what it may ultimately seem. The majestic nature of our existence has birthed a consciousness capable of self-creating this ancestral thirst for the truth. There is nothing wrong with attaching a motive for life to your presence, but it is when an individual settles with this flawed idea that they are stifling themselves from what it genuinely means to know the truth.

The truth exists all around us, as even our everyday lives bare all the evidence of how a world without a God would appear. It is up to the Christian to decide whether these are elements of reality or an accurate portrayal of a twisted system created by an all-powerful God. If we want to completely transform into a progressive civilization (intellectually, scientifically and socially), the necessity to carry on with the belief in God must be stricken from our collective judgment. Today in America, Christianity has caused an anti-advancing movement that will only produce a single outcome: a complete demurral in the direction that we ought to be heading in. Let me clarify by stating that this does not directly refer to our entirety in America, but within the hearts and minds of the believing individual, as that is where the solution exists. A change within them must take place before the more extensive issues can be laid to rest.

Once they free themselves from the progression-inhibitor that Christianity has planted, they'll finally experience what it means to be intelligently inclined. The absence of faith will produce a level of knowledge that can open the doors to a much more fascinating life than what Christianity has watered-down and structuralized. Their liberation from the strangle hold that has been imposed on the culture and society is key to our advancement into a future without the presence of an intellectually suicidal culture. Our very being is a testament to the integrity that is within us, but by believing in a 2000 year old dead Jewish middle-eastern that silently and vaguely watches over us will only tarnish the stage we are setting in place for those of the future. Though our society has been slowly digressing from the belief in God, a complete transformation from faith to reason must take place before we can socially evolve from infancy into rational maturity. God needs to go, and be forever gone.

DEFINING MY POSITION

"I'd take the awe of understanding over the awe of ignorance any day." - Douglas Adams, The Salmon of Doubt

I remember being only 16 years old when I was introduced to a much different form of religious instruction than I was before. I wasn't overtly religious; my faith in God was dismal at best. Yet, my belief persisted. Though in retro thought, it may've been because I was pandering to the beliefs of my girlfriend; a real big fan of Jesus. To please her, I attended a small Christian summer camp lasting no more than seven days. Regretful to say today, I volunteered a birthday present to visit this camp along with my girlfriend. I didn't care at the time; it made her happy and that was the business I was in at that time.

   I packed my bags and off I was. There was a good number of kids attending as well; perhaps 30 to 40 from what I can remember. A few my age but mostly young, around 10 and 12 years old. I remained reclusive, since socializing wasn't necessarily up my alley. My girlfriend and her friends were there, which was enough for me. The first day was quite casual, hanging around the camp mostly. It wasn't until the sun set did I realize what I was ultimately in for.

They gathered all the camp attendees and placed us in a room without ventilation. It being a late July night, you can imagine the atmosphere. The children were getting restless and I was growing tired of their childish antics; my patience was fleeting. It was then someone in the room noticed heat pouring from the vents. Soon, the room was damp, cramped, and unbearable. Eventually, perhaps 20 to 30 minutes later, we were let out. We were led across camp to the campus chapel where the leading pastor was waiting.

After we settled down, tired and drenched with sweat and confusion, he explained to us that what we experienced, the tremendous amount of stress and anguish, was Hell in recreation. That moment forever changed my outlook. It was no longer about the love of God or his relationship with us that I once thought so appealing; it was the fear of tormenting punishment in Hell that kept most Christians on their toes.

I recognize the absurdity in this. I thought, how ridiculous and petty does one have to be in resorting to tactics such as these? This wasn't the end of the babyish shenanigans. My girlfriend told me later that the older girls were forced to attend a meeting in which they discussed the "importance" of abstinence and that any form of sexual pleasure outside marriage was deemed evil in the eyes of Jesus. She even approached me, with tears in her eyes, and asked if we refrained from any form of whatever it was we were doing at that time – I will spare you the details. She was crying not because she was afraid of what I would say, but because she felt that here eternal soul was in jeopardy of burning in the fiery-pits of hell.

At the end of this whole mess, we were brought to the base of a steep hill. Eventually, camp counselors presented us with a large wooden cross. It was clear to me immediately; every one of us was forced to carry the cross – by ourselves – for a short period so we could feel the "tremendous burden" Christ carried during his last day of mortality. It was sad to watch the younger ones struggle, since there was nothing we were able to do. The trip concluded with the same, copy-and-paste style preaching we've listened to the entire camp stay.

I left the establishment in a different state of mind. It didn't bring enlightenment and it certainly didn't reinforce my "relationship" with God; I left with a tremendous question weighing down on me. It had nothing to do with my personal faith. It had everything to do with the actions and motivations of those inspired by their faith. At that moment I was still unaware of the crude and vile nature of the Bible, let alone the Koran. I still had yet to comprehend the intentions of those who perpetrated acts such as the Crusades, the Spanish Inquisition, the Salem Witch Trials, the purposeful cover-up by the Catholic Church of pedophile priests, and finally the September 11th attacks in New York City, D.C., and Pennsylvania. These, in my childish mind, didn't seem overtly religious in nature or even that those whom responsible did so with their faith and religious institution in mind.

Once this idea was impressed upon me, I reflected on my life with fear and animosity. Religion had played a significant role in my life and quite often the root of most of my anguish as a child. My ex-stepmother sometimes jokingly bolstered the phrase, "Spare the rod and spoil the child." Yet, it wasn't a joke; she often punished my sister in cruel fashions while I was subjected to a vile case of emotional pain. However amidst this pain, I still believed after all those years. Perhaps this was because I still believed I was "on the right side of the fence."

You see, when faith, even in its smallest of forms, still exists within the mind of a healthy person, you're still deluded of many things. In this particular case, I lacked to see the error of religion; the depravity and the degrading disposition it carried. Let it be known, however, that the claim religion is good for the world is false in nature and if one wishes to believe that to be true, they often do one of two things: either they attach the blame to the personal agenda of those behind the religious body or they express their belief that atheism has done much greater damage to humanity. Both, in my opinion, are foolish propositions.

For me to say that, I believe it's now my duty to defend my claim to the best of my abilities. Not because I feel as though the religious will come bearing torches and pitchforks, but because this sort of information is important. Most are as deluded as I once was. My only wish is to aid in ridding this world of bigotry, oppression, and as much violence as I can; and the best way to do this is to deny religion the respect so many believe it deserves. Christopher Hitchens once said, "I am absolutely convinced that the main source of hatred in the world is religion and organized religion. I am glad that you applaud, because it is a very great problem for those who oppose this notion, isn't it?" It certainly is.

Religion does indeed spoil the possibility of a prosperous future, which is why I'm so concerned. I fear at this point, the theist may suspect my arguments to be bias. Rest assured, their suspicions are in vain. Not because I haven't provided enough evidence of such, but because the evidence is in such abundance, in all of society. When we on the left side of the argument put forth supporting evidences, those on the right side often resort to vilifying our position; that atheism is somehow responsible for more terror and violence. In that claim, you'll notice a slight admission on the part of the religious. It is to say, "Yes, our religion – along with all other religions – are vile and contemptuous, but look how much worse your side is!" This should be acknowledged and those whom are responsible should be held responsible; and we mustn't let the religious dominate the landscape with such stupidity and ignorance. We must expose the wrongdoings on the part of the religiously inspired, because if it wasn't for their failings our species may've coexisted peacefully in the past and presumably continued to well into the future. That is our responsibility, once we've acknowledged this predicament.

At the same time, we should find solace and empowerment in the accomplishments of those who've stood against this wickedness both in the present and in the past. I will suggest that atheistic inspiration is the most powerful societal force, capable of much-needed reformation. If one hasn't, I believe embracing these powers with vigilance and courage we may see a world free from the disparaging effects of religion. Doing so will also halt and bring ruin to the detrimental forces of today, but this can only be done if we act as a single, unshakable unit. The promotion of reason is a necessity, particularly in a world dominated by superstition and ignorance.

Religion is no more useful than a wet hand towel; and where it has shown a glimmer of hope, those of faith have failed to prove that secular and atheist organizations are incapable of doing the same good work. On the other hand, religion has inspired many (from a few to a few million) to stand in defense of its wickedness. The rise of atheism is an inspiring and important tale, one which must be told. We atheists should be proud of those from our past who were willing to question the beliefs of institutionalized silliness.

From this, we should find the inspiration to work harder for a better tomorrow for those who still can't find the strength to come out as atheists. Of course, the previous statement doesn't reflect on the defects of the personality of the atheist. The only reason why these people can't come out is a reflection of the power of religion. If we find it imperative to help those in need, we must do what we can to extinguish the fire of religion. This very reason drives me as an author and blogger; and I won't stop until I cease to live.

CHAPTER ONE
AN ABSENT ETERNITY

"I would love to believe that when I die I will live again, that some thinking, feeling, remembering part of me will continue. But as much as I want to believe that, and despite the ancient and worldwide cultural traditions that assert an afterlife, I know of nothing to suggest that it is more than wishful thinking." - Carl Sagan, Billions and Billions

One of the key elements of the Christian doctrine is the existence of a beautiful, mind-calming spiritual destination where their soul will ultimately reside after death. Variations in the characteristics may differ from denomination to denomination, but the meaning behind the idea is generally the same. Once there, they will find themselves in the gracious company of Jesus Christ and his father. Their pain and suffering will cease and to be replaced by a calming sense of being. Their life has finally become complete, and their passage to eternity has been solidified. Everything they have been told during mass became true, and all their spiritual hard work finally paid off. With that being said, there exists no factual evidence for such a place to exist.

Scientists have studied this subject extensively and evidence suggests there to be no rational reason why consciousness would exist after death. Christians have proclaimed that such a place only resides in a spiritual realm untouchable by the hands of science. I would suggest that such an amazing notion would yield some sort of physical proof that could be testable. It's important to note that this firmament was once believed to be as real as you and I. But as man developed an understanding of the cosmos, the idea of a tangible heaven was erased. This flexibility will be something I will touch on later, but if mere men can change the nature of heaven, does that make God any more powerful than humans? These discrepancies about the essence of heaven stand as a testament to the flaws that exist within that portion of the Christian doctrine.

This cultural phenomenon has done a wonderful job of complicating these answers, with the use of unsubstantial anecdotal evidence. These claims are derived from a firsthand account taken at the brink of death, giving the witness a glimpse of what might lie just past that brilliant white light. Assertions such as a spiritual-based near death experience have influenced Christians into believing that eternal life may exist, while to scientists it has only demonstrated the actual capabilities of our own brain. It is a powerful mechanism, and to fully explain its complexity would take an inordinate amount of time. There have been significant advances within the past few decades that shine light on how our nervous system functions. As our understanding has progressed, so has the ability to conduct effective testing to explain things we cannot comprehend about our own physiology. Neuroscientists have dedicated much of their time to studying the validity of this mystifying claim, with some not-so-shocking results. In the simplest of explanations, our brains work as a massive electrical system. As we approach death, scientists have observed that our brains display neurons that fire at an incredible level. We can consciously absorb information or recall certain events after our heart stops for a short time with such vividness that one can confuse a natural experience for a spiritual one. The bright light at the end of the tunnel can also be explained quite bluntly. As your brain experiences blood loss, the functions of the eye begin to diminish. The vision narrows, all the while still absorbing the presence of illumination around you. It is absurd to think that a spiritual being is literally coaxing you to your demise.

One thing that ought to be considered is that this can only be experienced after the heart stops pumping but not after brain damage had set in; its given title is in effect quite appropriate because the patient isn't actually considered clinically dead. Another aspect that needs to be taken into account is the fact that many individuals all over the world slip out of life, only to be revived minutes later. Would it be so ignorant to inquire why a larger number of these patients do not display the same symptoms that the others have claimed? If this amazing and wonderful event had happened to a fraction of individuals, I would suggest that this would be a rather common occurrence, and it wouldn't be surprising to read of such reports. When doctors had finally been able to induce a patient's ability to experience one of these situations, it proved too many that this phenomena isn't as divine as one would have imagined. Christians and those with a belief in the supernatural will cast aside these scientific explanations and follow through with what they have always been taught: Faith trumps science.

I once had a friend describe a near-death experience where in which the patient, for some reason, had her eyes taped shut, yet she was able to describe her surroundings with fine precision. She exclaimed, "That just couldn't have been possible if she hadn't had an out-of-body experience!" Of course not, but she failed to see that what you're told just might not be exactly accurate. Her faith in the Christian religion was the nail in her coffin of reason. I gather that the modern Christian would accept these claims at face value because it validates what they've been told for years. The fact is that Christianity wasn't the first religion ever created, nor was it the first to propose an afterlife. What makes their claims any more accurate than another's claims? What has been more amazing than the experience itself is the cultural interest that this nation has taken in the post-death hypothesis.

To examine the events that are portrayed during a near-death experience, we must take a closer look at the social understanding that coexists with it. Most modern Christians living in the United States today have a very aesthetically pleasing image of heaven. It's often depicted as long, rolling pastures of green grass with a clear blue sky as a fitting backdrop. The sun always shines bright and the trees are lush with life. Who would not want to spend eternity in such a place as this? Coupled with this beautiful scenery, you'll be reunited with all of you long lost loved ones. Visual media has done a wonderful job of depicting this, giving them something to attach that belief to. This structured projection has morphed into something that has become sellable, much like a company changing the label on a product. It must standout and if done correctly, it will attract unknowing humans like a moth to a flame.

Everywhere we look, the existence of the paranormal has been demonstrated through television, cinema and literature. Numerous cable channels host television shows that depict the existence of an afterlife with outrageous claims that souls from deceased individuals walk this earth in a parallel universe that somehow only audio recording devices can intercept. Their evidence exists within their interpretation of photographs and audio clips. All of their results can be refuted when looked at skeptically. The fact that these assertions can be explained away ought to give the viewer or reader a clearer sense of what the reality of the paranormal really is. Anyone with an affirmed belief in the supernatural is only destroying their ability to rationally evaluate situations that seem confusing. The existence of ghosts lay in the mind of the believer and nowhere else does it dwell.

The Christian heaven has undergone many transformations throughout time. All following the same general scripture, each has interpreted it differently, creating their own from a fanciful imagination. The Lutheran denomination, that I once belonged to, promoted the mainstream variation of heaven, as I remember it being described. Their doctrine has made it quite easy to gain entrance, only needing to profess a belief in Jesus rather than play the waiting game only to discover you were not predestined to achieve eternal life. By lowering the bar and raising the appeal, it has made it quite enchanting. You must first think of the church as a business. Their tax exemptions are based solely on congregation attendance. If the average falls below a certain point, they will no longer be considered a religious institution and be forced to pay property tax. Also, the "donations" from the members contribute greatly toward the churches fund, so of course they would want to draw in the hapless individual.

The reason I am pointing this out ought to be somewhat blatant. They understand that there is a fear that surrounds death. Replacing that fear with anticipation is quite remarkable, and it's something they have done ridiculously well since the beginning of its institutionalization. Since its taken radical transformations to accommodate for a change in culture, this flexibility should not prove that God exists. It suggests that Christianity isn't as divinely inspired as once believed, since mere men have the ability to make decisions for an all-knowing God. So, how does a Christian decide that this was the chosen religion, with so many different variations of what happens to someone when they die? My ex-step mother belonged to the Jehovah's Witnesses, which has a drastically different take on the matter.

I remember only visiting their ceremonies on a few occasions but from those I was able to gather a good sense of what their doctrine held. They genuinely do not believe in any sort of an afterlife, which was quite astonishing to me at that time. There was no hell, no heaven, only a spiritual rapture that would take place upon Christ's return. How could this description bring about interest from the common individual? I was once told by her mother, that her own transition from Protestant took place when she learned that unbaptized children were sent to Hell in the event of their untimely demise. Along that line of logic, the existence of nothing seems more comforting than the possibility of spending the rest of eternity in a lake of fire. She thought she ought to double down and reaffirm her belief in God under a different jurisdiction to escape boundless punishment. While recalling this conversation, I was again reminded of the fear that Christianity fabricated within the believers mindset.

Once more, Christianity has created a problem while being the only one to offer the solution. Almost every Christian denomination has a varied version of heaven, but it should be noted that the sense of hell has always stayed consistent among them. The invention of hell and heaven in Christianity seems to only be a ploy to attract followers, using the sweet lure of eternal life to hook in the helpless while at the same time imposing the potentiality of burning in hell for not following. Think of what this can breed inside the believer's consciousness. If they wholeheartedly believe, then they would want the same for their loved ones. Once those loved ones are convinced, they would want that redemption for their loved ones. Christianity has truly created the greatest product known to man, and it's used a sort of multilevel marketing system as its model, founded on the imposition of fear. Christians often proclaim their good deeds lead them to salvation, and through those self-defined actions can one spend eternity with him. Though their motivation may be tainted with doctrine upon the description of their morality, they forget that social, cultural and evolutionary factors are what dictate our actions, not a divine individual with a key to heaven.

I do not need the fear of eternal punishment or the promise of eternal paradise to persuade me to treat others with respect and kindness. In death, there truly is nothing to fear. We will abruptly exit from this world just as swiftly as we came into being. The creation of our consciousness formed while we were developing in our mother's womb and its disappearance will occur upon our mortal exit. While not trying to refute religious belief, neuroscientists have done what they can to provide the evidence for this conscious mortality that Christianity has so desperately advocated against. There has been no credible proof put forth to suggest that a spiritual force provides life to our biological anatomy, so the existence of an afterlife must only be deemed as nonexistent. It has become nothing more than false hope created by those they've trusted to help give meaning to their lives. We are all pattern seeking individuals, and within this set pattern of life, some of us will never want to accept an end.

Much money has been made when individuals take advantage of those mourning the loss of loved ones. These people are known as psychic mediums that have a self-professed ability to speak with those beyond the grave. They have used basic intellectual manipulation to gather information so that they can obtain a good sense of whom or what the sufferer is missing. The problem with this ability is that there has been a lack of information provided to those who take these accounts seriously. Numerous individuals have made it quite clear how these con artists use deduction as a method to draw out certain emotions from those who are attending their services. Their actions have been regarded as fact based on the national consensus of belief that Americans maintain. It's appalling to witness so many hapless individuals taken advantage of in such a dubious fashion. It is a testament to how powerful the idea of the afterlife truly is, and how we are so refusing of the idea of mortality.

We sometimes regard ourselves as the greatest beings on Earth, even holding onto this view in the face of evidence demonstrating our fragile mortality. We can easily perish, while at the same time easily sustain life for great periods of time. This feeds the fear of death, since it can be so easily obtainable. People simply cannot accept that life is ending since we regard it with such reverence. Whether it is reincarnation, limbo, heaven, or a distant planet yet discovered, the afterlife is something we would all hope for. I wish there was somewhere after death that I could indulge in the company of my family, but there is not. I have accepted this fact, and with that I can live fruitfully. I do not take these days for granted, waiting for this trial period to end so I can move onto something greater. I realize that life is not about that. It is about living. I walk this earth with dignity, happiness and anticipation for the future. I love my family with all of my heart, and express that with the time I do have on this earth. Life is worth so much more than what has been portrayed to the Christian. You should love your family, do well by yourself and by others, and live your life to the fullest, because this one is the only one we're truly given.

Sources Used:

1. Lecher, Colin. "What Causes Near-Death Experiences?" Popular Science. http://www.popsci.com/science/article/2012-10/fyi-what-causes-near-death-experiences⌐

2. Levitan, Lynn and Stephen LaBerge. "Other Worlds: Out-Of-Body Experiences and Lucid Dreams" Nightlight 3, 1991.
   http://www.lucidity.com/NL32.OBEandLD.html

CHAPTER TWO
FLAWED LOGIC IN
MODERN MIRACLES

"Those of us who are proof against miraculous claims for the more obvious reasons-that the laws of nature do not respond to petitions and that what can be asserted without proof can be dismissed without proof-have a tendency to forget that this vulgarity and hysteria also increases the sum of misery on Earth, without at all diminishing it in the false promise of the afterlife." - Christopher Hitchens, Free Inquiry Magazine, Volume 24, Number 2

Throughout the bible, there are stories saturated with tales of prophets and priests performing miraculous tasks that defy what the ancient world would have considered normal. They witnessed unexplained plagues, parted seas, mass death, talking bushes, cured illnesses, food falling from the sky, men living inside of fish, walking on water, turning water into wine, men rising from the dead and ascending into heaven, and the list goes on and on. I will admit, these do seem quite spectacular but at the same time completely unrealistic. If the bible is a work of fiction, it is not out of the ordinary to speculate that these miracles were mere embellishments meant to bring awe to its readers. While it is very unlikely that these events actually happened, we often hear of completely random and self-fulfilling miracles happening all over the world today. Finding that the order of the universe is sometimes unimaginable, people with a Christian-based background tend to correlate these completely reasonable situations with the intervention of a higher power.

I've had my experience with a situation defined as "miraculous" by many of my theist relatives. It is up to you whether you will believe this or not. I am completely honest when retelling this story. I was in the fifth grade and on my way to school one spring morning. I lived in a small town in Illinois that was divided by a stretch of railroad tracks. Having lived on one side of them, I needed to cross them every morning to reach the bus stop. I approached these tracks on my bicycle and noticed to my right that an Amtrak train was barreling down on me. For whatever reason I decided to back pedal over the tracks and before I had realized, the train smashed into the front end of my bike, knocking me back almost 15 feet. I was alive without a scratch on my body. I remember my great-grandma telling me that I had angels watching over me and that God was on my side. I found it odd that they had bestowed this information unto me, because I knew the decision I made was a creation of my own self. My own survival was of my own doing, nothing divinely inspired compelled me to make those decisions. If my brain hadn't alerted my legs to back up, I could have been dead. In this, I found no good reason to chalk the circumstances of this event up to a god. If there had been a god, why hadn't he warned me of the train? For being as omnipotent and omnibenevolent as he is portrayed to be, he seems quite nonexistent where you would expect him to be.

As natural disasters seem to be waiting for us around every corner, death and dismay have become commonplace in news media. We're subjected to media coverage of massive floods, destructive tornadoes, and waste-laying hurricanes. The loss of innocent lives has been on the rise due to these events, but sometimes we're shown an example of God's "great acts." Whether it is a small puppy, an infant child, an elderly individual, or an untouched church or school, it appears that their god picks and chooses where he ought to shine his ever-loving light. Amidst the death of many and the enormous amount of damage done, the saving of one particular life seems to be extraordinary proof of a person's chosen theistic god. We all have seen television reports talking to local residence of a devastated neighborhood thanking their lord that they hadn't lost their lives. I've found this to be extremely telling of one's either indoctrination as a child or pure ignorance to reason. If I were faced with as much adversity as those victims were exposed to I would be asking God why he had done all of this damage in the first place. This all eventually ties into the claim that somehow God works in mysterious ways.

For the Christian, when looking at a perplexing situation, they are faced with a dilemma. They tend to avoid this internal conflict by explaining that God has a plan, and never will there be an understanding of that plan. If the claim can be explained in a completely natural and rational way, there certainly isn't anything mysterious about it. Sometimes we are faced with an example that can't be rationally explained, but there should be one aspect to consider. Why would such an impeccable being as God choose to work so elusively when he's made his presence quite clear throughout his holy book, moreover why would it be up to his sheepish followers to do the explaining? Of course, though, people have and always will proclaim that, "He" has touched their lives and hearts through his miraculous deeds; their ability to identify these "gifts" is based on an assumption collectively decided as self-satisfying when compared to any other options.

Prayer has been used by Christians much like a petition to pass a law. An increase in the number of prayers one receives, the higher the likelihood of something good occurring. Of course, these are usually directed toward a much less-fortunate human, sometimes suffering from a great illness or faced with poverty. There is one problem with this scenario, though. Prayer alone simply has never been proven to provoke a positive conclusion. Throughout this world, prayer is conducted every day on an exponential level, from every type of theist. One would imagine that a sudden increase of recovery would be demonstrated and that prayer would ultimately be proven to work as a remedy. Yet, we don't see doctors writing a prescription for "1 to 2 prayers per day distributed orally." Prayers are conducted and people still suffer every day. This ought to be enough proof to show that it simply does not work as a viable treatment.

Sometimes, however, patients do suddenly recover. At the same time, they were also receiving some sort of medical care. This biased understanding within the Christian may see this in a completely different way. An example of this would be a terminal cancer patient with an expected life of 3 to 6 months beating the cancer successfully. Someone praying for this individual would see this as confirmation that their uplifted internal conscious muttering had somehow wormed its way into their medical treatments. My issue with this is that it removes one from owing the proper gratitude to the correct individual. Instead of thanking the doctors and his team for the healing of their loved one, they thank a god for the hard work done. At the same time, they have forgotten they are thanking the very god that allowed that person to receive the terminal cancer in the first place. It's all very perplexing when actually looked at from a different perspective, isn't it? Apart from these rather moderate examples of miraculous occurrences, there exists a much more ludicrous and absurd observation.

We've all laughed at the man or woman seeing Jesus' face on a piece of pizza. However, people truly do look at these ridiculous notions through their faithfully accepting eyes. There have been many over-sensationalized examples of miracle work throughout the decades. One of which is the well-known "stigmata." Stigmata occurs when a believing individual physically bares the wounds that Christ himself sustained during the crucifixion. While hearing the tales of those experiencing this baffling infliction, we're often excluded from any skeptical and factual conclusions. I remember hearing of this as child and wondering how this could have occurred. Of course, as a child I didn't ask the appropriate questions. First, was this inflicted by the individual themselves? Secondly, did the patient suffer from a mental illness that could have been attributed to the cause of this? Case studies and research have shown that a resounding "yes" could be answered for both. The sufferer has generally been proven to be guilty of perpetrating the actual inflictions, done so for either attention or because their mental illness led them to do so. For whatever reason it may be, it still demonstrates that there has never been a conclusive case of stigmata to show a supernatural origin. Something

18

else to be noted is that the wound on the palm of the individual is typical of most contemporary and medieval art depicting the crucifixion. Some historians believe that when crucifixions took place nails were often driven into the wrist between the radius and ulna bone to help stabilize the individual. If God were to impose such marks on a believer, wouldn't it be logical that he'd at least be accurate? That may be too much to ask for, though.

Of course, there have been other examples of faith-based mass delusions categorized as miracles. Another popular example is that of crying statues, where religious figures seem to manifest tears of water or blood from their eyes. Sometimes, when one is exposed to these fanciful stories there is a key element that if often left out: The conclusion. Almost all the documented cases were verified as hoaxes, usually perpetrated by the individual responsible for the statue. These have shown that deliberate manipulations are to blame, being either paint or actual human blood. Naturally, thousands of believers would flock from miles around to gaze upon the wonderful miracle bestowed upon them. What drives so many individuals to cast aside logic so easily? Christian faith is to blame, where the absence of reason is somehow regarded as valuable. Debunking seems to make little difference when putting these ludicrous claims to rest. If your doctor was prescribing you a drug that hasn't been proven to heal your illness, would you still swallow that pill? Of course not! If such claims have been proven to be false since the beginning, what gives someone the reason to believe subsequent accounts? It's irritating to see such an intelligent race constantly being fooled by such obvious manipulations.

The need of miracle work all goes back to one central argument: People have always needed something to believe in. Their faith has been pounded into their subconscious their entire lives, allowing the line between reality and fantasy to be blurred. Their lives are often formed around their religious beliefs, so it isn't uncommon to see them draw such illogical conclusions. People claim to witness the appearance of their god in almost anything they wish to see him in. Christopher Hitchens was right when he explained that god was real, but only in the mind of the believer. This is called confirmation biasness, when they wishfully hope for something to occur and when it comes to fruition in a completely logical way, there will always be the attachment of divine intervention. I'm sure there is a Christian somewhere right now, praying that my atheism be stricken from me and may I be bathed in the body and blood of Christ. There will be no such thing occurring, because it does not work. Miracles have been used in literature to separate the subject from normalcy, making them above us somehow. That was when there hadn't been any way to prove anything to the contrary. The more rationally we developed, the more we began to see the logical fallacies that existed in the mind of the believer. God has always been described as mysterious, but yet he decides to only appear when convenient for him. He saves one human life every so often, while also providing completely natural explanations for what he supposedly did.

Today there isn't a need for miracles, because science has replaced wishful thinking with hard work and determination. If you witness something outside the realm of your understanding, do not explain it away by owing it to an invisible being. An appropriate answer ought to be sought out to determine if a super-duper space god is deserving of that recognition. If an individual, or their loved ones, discovers themselves sick, mentally anguished, or desperate for nourishment, they shouldn't rely on a prayer-induced miracle. I will guarantee them there will be no such rapture from those devastating occurrences. Just because 1 out of 1000 people survives a doomed prognosis does not give you a viable reason to suggest that it was the work of God. Miracles have proven to be nothing more than supernatural reasoning behind something with completely naturalistic explanations, and that is the extent of it.

Sources Used:

1. A debate between Christopher Hitchens and William Lane Craig titled "Does God Exist?" at Biola University in April of 2009.

CHAPTER THREE
THE ERROR IN FAITH-BASED MORALITY

"With or without religion, you would have good people doing good things and evil people doing evil things. But for good people to do evil things, that takes religion." - Steven Weinberg, from the Conference on Cosmic Design in April of 1998

Christians have used their sense of morality to separate themselves from a world filled with mentally corrupt individuals. Their religion has taught them that their action towards others have a divine origins, a gift given to them by their lord. When individuals begin to claim their sense of right and wrong is spiritually created, they neglect to consider any other elements that may play a larger role. In fact, the answer is quite colorful. A religious believer can claim that their innate drive to show compassion is a blessing unto them from God till their heart's content, but the fact is that it purely isn't the case. Having been indoctrinated as a species for a few thousand years, religion has staked its claim on the debate of the origin of morality. With that, however, comes something that requires questioning, criticism and finally disregard.

When looking at the human race collectively, we've found a way to work together and properly influence others. Except for certain religiously based societies, many of the secular nations display a sense of right and wrong that has allowed them advance in a positive way. Where does this social drive exist that promotes equality and functioning goodness? We, as humans, strive for social acceptance. Sometimes with that we find certain characteristics that one may describe as moral, as well as immoral. We feel the need to fit in, and those regulations can bring about alternative definitions for what we consider right and wrong. I can personally describe a situation where I had actually allowed myself to lower my standards for others to find acceptance. In high school, I was considered arrogant, and rightly so. I found entertainment in ridiculing others. I did so to show to my peers that I was worthy of friendship. I sincerely apologize to those I've hurt, and deeply regret my actions. I remember feeling bad for those I degraded, but the need for acceptance was overwhelming. This all eventually led to an awakening brought about by the news of a young teenager that attempted suicide; a boy I often teased. Ever since, I've always tried to make an effort in reforming my past tendencies. From my experience, a sense of right and wrong can greatly differ based on social constitutions. When we look at social communities, there exists a set of moral guidelines they ought to adhere to. This had been collectively decided by the community for the sole purpose of either advancing their race or conserving their ideals. This flexibility that we find among different cultures all has a naturalistic root. Within our genetic code, there exists an ancestral answer that is much more intriguing.

Evolutionary biologists believe that our raw ability to tell right from wrong is a by-product of our ancestral DNA. If our ancient predecessors hadn't acknowledged that killing one other was detrimental to the progress of our species, we would have died off millions of years ago. We are a social species with the need to associate with other individuals to advance in many different ways, so the need to collectively get along is imperative to our survival. Ancient people were mystified by their innate ability to treat others with respect, using some sort of god to explain this confusing instinct. Without having the ability to understand the science behind it, their only option was to attach this biological question with that of their religious beliefs. This lack of understanding today can only be attributed to an individual's religious faith, which has kept them from seeking the appropriate answers. Christians believe that their sense of morality has been given to them by their god, and since it has been given to them by an omnipotent being, it can't be questioned. Well, I believe it ought to be. Why would anyone with an ounce of dignity and humility stand behind a god that displayed as much anger, rage, and destruction as he has demonstrated? When we take a closer look at the holy books that describe actions according to God's ideals, we find a sense of faith-based morality that directly conflicts any morality that promoted social progression.

Within the Christian bible, the Old Testament displays situations that if witnessed today would be considered appalling and disturbing. Senseless acts of violence, tribal warfare and illogical law exist within the confines of the Torah, something that seems to have been forgotten by modern Christians. After one decides to read the scripture through an objective lens, the results may seem quite shocking. As a child, I rarely, if ever, gave much thought about the stories I was read. Now that I look at this in a more objective sense, I'm amazed that I hadn't picked up on it much sooner. Though Christians have identified this holiday with Christ, one example is that of the Passover. Looking back, I only remember this occasion as a time when which God had demonstrated his final act that lead to the departure of the Jews from the stranglehold of the Egyptians. To be Biblically accurate, the Jews were commanded to wipe the blood of a recently slain lamb over the top of their door so that the god's spirit would know not to kill the first born son of that specific family. I wish I had the voice I have today, because I would have questioned everything I found to be confusing. If their lord was able to mercilessly kill without hesitation, why must he be regarded as so loving and caring? This is not the beginning, or end for that matter, of the detestable nature that was demonstrated by their "loving" God.

Evidence of this can be found in the beginning chapters of the bible. According to the book of Genesis, the humans that God had created became so appalling that he decided to do away with them and start fresh. His anger is brought to fruition when a raging flood roared through the land, killing every living thing except for Noah and his family as he had promised. For being superior to humans he displays many of our most lowly regarded emotions, such as anger, rage, and contempt. We look down upon people who let their anger get the best of them, yet Christians look at this without hesitation. Later on, he commands Abraham to offer his son Isaac as an offering unto him. Abraham's willingness and acceptance of god allows him to follow through with the command. As he is about to murder his son, God stops him after Abraham demonstrated what God wanted proved to him. I can only imagine the fear that seethed inside Isaac as his father was about to slay him. Though he hadn't actually murdered his son, God could have gotten his answer in a much more constructive and less destructive manner.

In the book of Exodus, we're given samples of discipline provided by their god. Here are examples of such biblical accounts.

"When a man strikes his male or female slave with a rod so hard that the slave dies under his hand, he shall be punished. If, however, the slave survives for a day or two, he is not to be punished, since the slave is his own property." - Exodus 21:20-21

Modern apologists maintain that God never allowed the owning of slaves, but if you do find yourself owning one, this was how you ought to have treated them. If God hadn't allowed those men to own slaves, why would they include laws regarding the owning of one? If their god found it to be moral to inconsiderately beat their slaves to the brink of death, I find there to be nothing omnibenevolent about him. This type of logical fallacy is known as "special pleading", something that Christians do regularly and unknowingly. The next passage one may find to be awfully disturbing.

"When a man sells his daughter as a slave, she will not be freed at the end of six years as the men are. If she does not please the man who bought her, he may allow her to be bought back again. But he is not allowed to sell her to foreigners, since he is the one who broke the contract with her. And if the slave girl's owner arranges for her to marry his son, he may no longer treat her as a slave girl, but he must treat her as his daughter. If he himself marries her and then takes another wife, he may not reduce her food or clothing or fail to sleep with her as his wife. If he fails in any of these three ways, she may leave as a free woman without making any payment." - Exodus 21:7-11

Could you imagine selling your daughter into a macabre sex-slave trading business? Well, apparently God had. We find this action to be unimaginable today. We all have watched news stories detailing the horrors and violence that women as sex slaves endure. Any God who condones this type of act ought to be shunned just as we would the actual offender. It is disgusting to think doing something such as that to my own daughter. This type of misogynistic behavior is not the extent of it.

"You shall not allow a sorceress to live." - Exodus 22:18

This type of religious instruction has brought pain and anguish to those who defied them. Something still relatively fresh in history is that of the Salem Witch Trials. Many women were wrongly convicted of having taken part in witchcraft. Using the bible when deciding how to punish them, the court system decided that swift death by burning was the only option. Faith-based morality, again, demonstrated its adverse effects within that small society. Without the bible, I don't believe those individuals would have come to such an extravagant conclusion. Many innocent lives wouldn't have been lost if there hadn't been an allowance given in their chosen holy book.

"Whoever lies with an animal shall be put to death." - Exodus 22:19

Bestiality wasn't understood then as a condition that can be prevented if taken the proper precautions. Why would god allow an individual to kill someone that sometimes never had an option with the situation? It only makes sense if we understand that the people who wrote the bible merely looked at this action with disgust and found it to be worthy of death. Later, there existed even more illogical injunctions that seem to omit any sense of reason.

Leviticus is considered God's book of laws, but not regarded as so by mainstream Christians. Here are some examples from within its pages:

"For every one who curses his father or his mother shall be put to death; he has cursed his father or his mother, his blood is upon him." - Leviticus 20:9

The murder of disobedient children is unimaginable. Sometimes they are born with inflictions that can't be prevented. We understand today that certain mental conditions never allow a child to grow to the mental capacity that a normal human would. There isn't a logical explanation for why God would allow these children to be killed knowing wholeheartedly that it may not have been their fault. In America, there even exists a sense of morality within prisons when it comes to child murderers. They are dealt with swiftly. How is it that convicted criminals have somehow collectively decided on a moral conviction that even surpasses that of God?

Within that book, God also instructs the killing of priests who leave the temple without permission. The priest is also to be murdered if he drinks an alcoholic beverage. Apparently those who decided to use wine as a metaphor when conducting communion must have missed this little tid-bit of information. Death must be dealt out to those who sleep with their own mother, those who sleep with their daughter-in-law, the daughters of priests who practice fornication, blasphemers and adulterers. Why must death be the final solution? Why can't these acts be dealt with so that those who commit them learn from their mistakes rather face imminent death? What I've never understood is that our modern-day society has somehow found a way to be morally superior to God in almost every aspect imaginable.

The litany of stupidity is endless, and these situations merely expose God as immorally equal to that of Hitler and Stalin. What needs to be brought to light is their motivation for explaining away the detestable legislation passed forth by God. Jesus is touted by Christians as loving, compassionate, and just. His teachings and lessons outlined in the Gospels describe a man of love, forgiveness, and strength. With this, they believe that Jesus had abolished the old laws with an entirely new covenant built with humility and forgiveness. However, Jesus spoke plainly about his agenda, which consisted of upholding his father's previous laws, as demonstrated in the book of Matthew.

"Do not think that I have come to abolish the Law or the Prophets; I have not come to abolish them but to fulfill them." - Matthew 5:17

This type of cherry-picking is what allows Christians to decide on a faith-driven sense of right and wrong. When looking at the scripture there exists directions that I would refuse to accept if I were a believer. Jesus asserts to his followers that if they find themselves distracted by their families, they are to cast them aside for him. If I were to leave my wife today for the sole purpose of spiritual acceptance, I would never forgive myself. The love I have for her would greatly outweigh any sense of obligation I would have for any godly being. When compared to our current moral understanding, Jesus has proven himself to be quite the contrary.

Morality, in the sense of having a divine origin, can be completely selfish in nature. If Christians are doing right by others and only doing so to reserve their spot in heaven, there ought to be no reason to take such individuals seriously. There is no valuable morality found within a doctrine that requires it for the sole purpose of self-satisfaction and redemption. When I make a decision that requires a regard for either human life or the dignity of others, I do not do so with a personal agenda. I do so because it is important to treat others with respect and love. We all have blood that flows through our veins and air that is taken in by our lungs.

We inhabit the same celestial body that roars through space at a tremendous speed. We are all human. With that, I find reasoning for my morality. I accept that it may have an evolutionary base, but from that I am able to build from. I am not guided by a book that displays acts of destruction and hate. I do not possess a higher power that habitually taunts me with the possibility of eternal damnation. I work in accordance to the respect I have for other individuals. When their personal salvation is deemed more important that the well-being of their fellow humans, they've set themselves back generations from where we are today. If they claim their morality is derived from their chosen theistic belief, I urge them to reconsider those ideas and decide whether it truly is moral to be as selfish and blind as their religion requires them to be.

Sources Used:

1. FitzPatrick, William. "Morality and Evolutionary Biology", The Stanford Encyclopedia of Philosophy (summer 2012 Edition) http://plato.stanford.edu/entries/morality-biology/ ⊏

2. Louis-Jacques, Lyonette. "The Salem Witch Trails: A legal bibliography" University of Chicago: Library News. 10-29-2012. http://news.lib.uchicago.edu/blog/2012/10/29/the-salem-witch-trials-a-legal-bibliography-for-halloween/

CHAPTER FOUR
THE MYTH OF CREATION

"Evolution could so easily be disproved if just a single fossil turned up in the wrong date order. Evolution has passed this test with flying colours." - Richard Dawkins, The Greatest Show on Earth: The Evidence for Evolution

The origin of life is something that has mystified humans for a number of centuries. From the time of the Sumerians, we know that humans have struggled to answer this baffling question. Every early civilization with a theistic idea has an origin story of some sort, each giving the believer a level of comfort and sense of purpose about the order of this universe. However, many of those daunting questions have been answered through the determination of our most brilliant minds. Science has progressed so much so that many of the dense religious creation notions have either been flat-out proven wrong or at a certain level deemed illogical. Our understanding of this natural world far surpasses anything proposed by a theistic belief, yet there exists a level of misunderstanding still going on today. To simply disregard all that has been discovered by our most prominent scientists is absurd, foolish and detrimental. With as much evidence for evolution that has been exposed, I see no reason why an intelligent person could believe that a transcendental and supernatural being had any part in its creation.

On numerous occasions, I have been asked if I believe, "We crawled out of a pond somewhere and here we are?" The level of astonishment that grew was almost unbearable. I would promptly answer, "Simplistically, yes." This told me that there is an educationally flawed discourse that exists within the confines of this country's borders. The problem that we face comes from the time the idea is planted into our fragile minds. If an individual is told that all living creatures were created by God at an early enough age, they could potentially vest all of their intelligence into this notion and could more easily cast aside any ideas that may refute that claim. The first time I remember being taught any sort of evolutionary biology was in my initial biology course I was required to take during high school. By then, it is safe to say that most of my peers would have already decided on a solution for why the world is the way that it is. I was taught God was the ultimate creator before the school system had a chance to explain the idea of evolution at its most simplistic level.

When looking at the order in which a fetus grows within its mother's womb and the stages a human progresses through until reaching full maturity, I can easily see why any uneducated individual can find the existence of God within the molecules that we are consisted of. Evolution is as complex as it is erroneous. It does not follow a predetermined set of instructions. It is the reason many of our ancestors are extinct, but it's also why I am here typing this out. Ever since Charles Darwin first considered the idea of natural selection, scientists have compounded on that notion with evidence from a tangible level to a cellular level. They've mapped the genetic codes of numerous species to identify the origin of their most basic survival traits. Most of those who dispute the claim of evolution can't simply agree that we are all apes, in more ways than imaginable. It quite confusing why this is so readily cast aside, while the idea of a man created of dirt and a woman created from a rib is somehow more logical.

One of the most absurd questions proposed by creationists is "If we evolved from monkeys, why are there still monkeys?" They often snicker when asking, thinking they've figured out the "got-ya" question. The infantile nature of that question only suggests that they lack any sort of knowledge about our biological lineage. We are not the highest product of a scripted creation. The fossil record alone has proven that we weren't always the only ape-like creatures that walked upright. Our existence on earth was solely based on the biological divergence that happened among the Homo Heidelbergensis that also brought life to what we would consider the Neanderthal. Before all of this, evidence from the fossil record has painted the simple tale of our biological progress.

About 25 million years ago a hominid from Africa would face a series of genetic mutations that would bring about the existence of the monkey, orangutan, gorilla, chimpanzee and eventually the Homo Sapiens. From there, a series of minor genetic mutations, sparked by environmental changes, would occur that would bring about the modern man.

It is widely believed that humans first migrated out of Africa, possibly due to naturalistic causes, around 100,000 years ago. The evidence for this has been determined by a complete reconstruction of the human genome. Using this method, they've hypothesized that a small cluster of humans left Africa by crossing the Red Sea, expanding into Europe and Asia some time later. From Asia, some traveled down into the islands of Papua New Guinea then on to Australia. Others from Asia traveled east up toward Russia, eventually crossing the frozen ice bridge between Europe and the Americas roughly 15,000 years ago. From there they traveled south, some travelling across Canada, others travelling down the United States and finally resting in South America. This entire process took approximately 98,000 years to complete entirely. History has told us that roughly 5,000 years ago Sumerians were the first to develop writing, while earlier hominids already developed tools that accommodated their everyday lives. That allows for the previous 95,000 years of evolutionary changes among the Homo Sapiens to enhance communication skills such as script and speech. Our capabilities are not a product of the Tower of Babel, but of tens of thousands of years of developing intelligence. What we know today is only a blink in the eye of this world, so we should not limit our understanding within a 6,000 year period, which is exactly what creationists do.

Their ideas have been disregarded by the scientific community for the most obvious reasons. Their understanding of modern science has been distorted due to their ignorant eye constructed by their religious beliefs. There ought not to be a rational reason why humans today can honestly believe that God created this world 6000 years ago. They find it completely feasible that male and female members of the 85 million species that exist on this earth were able to fit on a wooden ship the size of a football field. They also believe that humans lived well into their 900s. This is all ridiculous, but the one thing that has always baffled me was their claim that the evidence of intelligent design can be found within every living thing on earth, particularly us. They claim that our anatomical system is so complex that only something with great brilliance could have constructed such a beautiful being. When in reality, there is more evidence to prove the exact opposite of that notion.

We are all the same type of beings, differing by only 1% of our actual DNA. Within this DNA that we all share, there exist parts of that structure that are no longer functional, because our evolutionary timeline has decided that they are no longer useful. Humans all over the planet have been born with what we consider a "tail." While most cases suggest that there lacks any vertebrae within these fleshy extensions, it has told scientists that these may have existed among our ancestral predecessors. Another part of our anatomy that is no longer functioning is the appendix. While other smaller mammals seem to have a use for this organ, we have evolved past its once apparent need. Today, its only function seems to pose a threat to our health if there is a rupture. We all have visited the dentist office one time or another and were graciously told about the need to remove our wisdom teeth so that infection can be averted. We once needed these to help grind up course vegetation but as we've biologically evolved, our jaw sizes changed due to an adjustment in our diet. These are just a few of the many indicators that we were once very different mammals than we currently are today. Why would these exist if there seems to be no important need for them? This does not seem so "intelligent" to even a simple human as I.

These types of ancestral remnants not only exist within our own anatomy, they also exists within all types of animals on this planet. Within the Killer Whale remain certain artifacts left over from when it once was a land dwelling creature. There are fragments of bone that suggests that a girdle for a hind pelvic bone once existed. Even inspection of the bone structure of any whale's forelimb bears a staggering resemblance to that of a quadruped animal. When looking at the anatomy of a giraffe, Richard Dawkins brought to light the laryngeal nerve in his book, The Greatest Show on Earth. He explained that this nerve took an unusual route, needing only to travel from the brain to the larynx, where in actuality it leaves the brain and travels down into the chest cavity and back toward the larynx. This detour is persistent among mammals, but in giraffes this nerve travels a total of 13 feet to reach its destination only inches from the starting point. Biologists suggest this is because of the evolutionary path fish took to become mammals. If a creator truly designed this animal, why take such an extravagant detour when constructing this creature? These examples are often overlooked by the common creationists, who tend to stick to more superficial examples when trying to prove the existence of a powerful creator.

They claim that the structure of the eye is so intricate that evolution simply could not have constructed such a functioning organ. While on the surface this notion doesn't seem plausible, biological studies have shown that the eye was not a sudden creation, but has been evolving for millions of years. Darwin recognized the importance of the eye when determining the survival rate of species. It is logical to assume that a species with lesser eye sight are more likely to go extinct while species with better eye sight may flourish. As a result, in most cases the eye has taken the proper steps to ensure that its species would survive. While some animal species haven't attained this evolutionary benefit, other aspects of their anatomy have allowed them the ability to survive. Bats have terrible eye sight when compared to other animals, but they've adapted to their surrounds by using sonar as a way to hunt for appropriate food. It would be ignorant to suggest that all the animals on earth with different types of visionary avenues were all created as is, because the evidence strongly confirms that the eye has changed time and time again.

Often regarded as irrational, creationists believe that dinosaurs once existed amongst humans, and were explicitly mentioned within the bible. There extinction was a product of the biblical flood as depicted in the book of Genesis. There hasn't been any scientific evidence to suggest that a biblical flood ever took place, and that dinosaurs ever coexisted with hominids nonetheless. Their push for these answers have driven them to the corners of the earth, funding explorations into the jungles of Africa where they have attempted to find living proof of a supposed brontosaurus-type animal named Mokele-Mbembe by local tribesman. They've also widely popularized the Paluxy prints, which were once speculated to have been dinosaur tracks with human tracks running parallel with them. George Adams was the first man to have made this claim, but since it has been acknowledged as a hoax. In the face of adversity, they muster the courage to press forward, even attempting to popularize these ideas with faith-based museums. "Creationist Museums" have been constructed all over the world, displaying only litany of factual errors. It's disturbing to imagine that the majesty of this world has been destroyed by those who refuse to believe anything different from what they've been told as children. Their unnerving stance is actually quite impressive, because it takes an immense amount of faith to believe something like this without the evidence.

Creationists are finding it harder and harder to explain away the preponderance of evidence against their views. They've manipulated their previous ideas to accommodate this intellectual dilemma they've found themselves in. Instead of accepting evolution as a whole, they've claimed that God created proto-species and allowed microevolution to exist. Many moderate Christians in America have even adjusted their belief so much so that the stories are allegorical, completely separating themselves from the scientific community all together. Within the past decades, creationists have attempted to impose their faith-based views on those with a more impressionable sense of reality.

The teaching of creationism has been debated for some time, often resulting in high court trials. The very first case brought to the Supreme Court was that of Epperson vs. Arkansas in 1968, where the teaching of evolution was first disputed. The court found that evolution could not be banned, nor could it be restricted on the grounds of religious doctrine. In 1994, the Seventh Circuit Court of Appeals ruled in favor of the New Lenox School district prohibiting a teacher from teaching creationism alongside evolution. Many other vain attempts have been made but almost all have been met with failure. This is why most Christians that share such a strong creationist view tend to home school their children, using the immoral tools provided to them by websites like Answers in Genesis. 38% of all homeschooled children are in the position that they are in because of their parent's decision to rear them with a Christian education. While this is ultimately the parent's choice, it is still a biased approach to the national curriculum that ought to stay unbiased to promote universal learning. Instead, this approach hinders a child's knowledge of the reality of the natural world.

Historical and evolutionary evidence has proven creationism to be only a myth among the intellectually superior. The proof of evolutionary life exists all around us, and with the slightest glance at this world will yield all the answers. Religion is the only thing stopping humanity from fully grasping the idea of the natural world. Creationists are free to believe that the earth is anywhere from 9,000 to 6,000 years old, 170 million animals could fit on one ship, and humans could live for almost a millennium. Even in the face of evidence that ultimately removes any divine guidance perpetrated by God, they are free do what they wish within their own mental framework. The problem arises when their radical, fundamental approach to the subject becomes infectious. They attack the potential intelligence of a child and infect their minds with unproven hypotheses and describe them as fact.

Children are fragile and susceptible to any sort of pressure. Preservation of faith is their driving motive, and by doing so they maintain a sense of intellectual hierarchy that they feel separates them from the rest. Of course, their assumptions are ludicrous, illogical, and implausible. Creationism and its fallacious nature need to be maintained within the mind of the believer, and there it needs to stay.

Sources Used:

1. O'Neil, Dr. Dennis. "Homo heidelbergensis", Evolution of Modern Humans.

http://anthro.palomar.edu/homo2/mod_homo_1.htm

2. Dawkins, Richard. "The Fifth Ape." The Genius of Charles Darwin. Channel 4. August of 2008.

3. Faculty of Oriental Studies. "Sumerian Language" ETCSL Language.03-29-2005.
    http://etcsl.orinst.ox.ac.uk/edition2/language.php

4. National Human Genome Research Institution "Frequently Asked Questions about Genetic and Genomic Science".
    https://www.genome.gov/19016904

5. "Whales Had Legs, Wiggled Hips, Study Says." Daily Nature and Science News and Headlines | National Geographic News. N.p., n.d. 9-11-2008 http://news.nationalgeographic.com/news/2008/09/080911-whale-legs.html⊏

6. Dawkins, Richard. The Greatest Show on Earth: The Evidence for Evolution. Free Press, New York. 2010.

7. Darwin, Charles. The Origin of Species. New York: P.F. Collier & Son, 1937.

8. Kuban, Glenn, and Gregg Wilkerson. "The "Burdick Print"" The Burdick Print.
   http://paleo.cc/paluxy/wilker6.htm

9. Epperson v. State of Arkansas, Supreme Court of the United States, 1968, 393 U.S. 97, 89 S. Ct 266 and 917 F2d 1004 Webster v. New Lenox School District No M as described in the portion "A Lost Cause"

CHAPTER FIVE
AN IMAGINARY END

"The fact that religions can be so shamelessly dishonest, so contemptuous of the intelligence of their adherents, and still flourish does not speak very well for the tough-mindedness of the believers. But it does indicate, if a demonstration was needed, that near the core of the religious experience is something remarkably resistant to rational inquiry." - Carl Sagan, Broca's Brain

The New Testament is filled to the brim with assertions of the second coming, when we would personally witness the second coming of Jesus Christ himself. He'll ride from the heavens on the back of a majestic white horse, saving those who believe and damning those who do not. Those alive will join him in Heaven while others who have passed will be contently waiting for their arrival. Christians will proclaim today that Armageddon is upon us, based on the status of our planet. As the population rises, wars and famine have ensued. Catastrophic weather patterns, most recently Hurricane Sandy, have brought about destructive storm systems that ravage the land of this world, causing death to the less fortunate and turmoil for those who survive. The Antichrist and his climb to power have been pointed out by Christians as taking place today. The error within this litany of speculation is its redundant nature. It's important to recognize that these claims have been made for centuries, all producing neither the end of the world or Christ's second arrival. Of course, each generation has their own answers for why they believe the world will end. Even the bible itself contended that Armageddon would happen within the following decades of its composition, as demonstrated in the book of Luke. Why would an all-powerful being take such drastic steps to turn this life we live into some sort of live-action game meant for his amusement? If he has the power, why hasn't it happened yet if promised so long ago? It's ridiculous to wait for a rapture that clearly hasn't been demonstrated to be a viable event. The only evidence that Christians can use to make such an assertion come from their Bible, which has proven to be a problematic as their line of reasoning.

Christianity has had a horrible history of foretelling the rapture. Their claims are doused in evidence derived from cultural influences and scriptural passages and while as insane as this may sound, these people have, and still do, honestly believe the notions they are asserting. Their ultimate problem lies within the texts that they so avidly uphold. As true as the Bible has been claimed to be, there exists discrepancies and convenient alternations pertaining to the second coming that ought to be recognized by any rational person.

The book of Daniel details his premonitions given to him by God, describing the events that are to unfold before the messiah makes his final return. There are many correlations that can be made between his prophecies and the writings in the New Testament. Daniel spoke of the destruction of the temple in Jerusalem, as did Jesus in the book of Mark.

"After the sixty-two 'sevens,' the Anointed One will be cut off and will have nothing. The people of the ruler who will come will destroy the city and the sanctuary. The end will come like a flood: War will continue until the end, and desolations have been decreed." Daniel 9:26

"As Jesus was leaving the temple, one of his disciples said to him, "Look, Teacher! What massive stones! What magnificent buildings!" "Do you see all these great buildings?" replied Jesus. "Not one stone here will be left on another; every one will be thrown down."" - Mark 13:1-2

He also made claims that can be correlated with the stories told within Revelations, such as the beast that is to bring about the return of the messiah.

"The beast I saw resembled a leopard, but had feet like those of a bear and a mouth like that of a lion. The dragon gave the beast his power and his throne and great authority. One of the heads of the beast seemed to have had a fatal wound, but the fatal wound had been healed. The whole world was filled with wonder and followed the beast. People worshiped the dragon because he had given authority to the beast, and they also worshiped the beast and asked, 'Who is like the beast? Who can wage war against it?'" - Revelation 13:2-4

"In the first year of Belshazzar king of Babylon, Daniel had a dream, and visions passed through his mind as he was lying in bed. He wrote down the substance of his dream. Daniel said: "In my vision at night I looked, and there before me were the four winds of heaven churning up the great sea. Four great beasts, each different from the others, came up out of the sea." - Daniel 7:1-3

Daniel then goes on to elaborate about the final beast he witnessed.

"After that, in my vision at night I looked, and there before me was a fourth beast—terrifying and frightening and very powerful. It had large iron teeth; it crushed and devoured its victims and trampled underfoot whatever was left. It was different from all the former beasts, and it had ten horns. While I was thinking about the horns, there before me was another horn, a little one, which came up among them; and three of the first horns were uprooted before it. This horn had eyes like the eyes of a human being and a mouth that spoke boastfully." Daniel 7:7-8

My problem with these correlations is that they are taken at face-value by the believer. They assume these are the words of God. I am under the belief that men wrote these now-famous texts, which raises some red flags for me. When Christianity was developing, the creation of a messiah and his return needed to be fulfilled. This would have forced the writers to turn to the Torah to rectify some of the unanswered questions derived from it, which is being done today. It is completely logical to assume that some of the New Testament teachings of an Armageddon were nothing more than fanciful elaborations conducted by their dubious writers.

Jesus himself hinted at his eventual return throughout the Gospels. Many end-times prophesiers directly cite those texts as proof of validity for their ridiculous claims. Jesus is touted as the son of God, perfect and impeccable. Yet, he had found a way to contradict himself on numerous occasions. When examining the error within those texts, it's only rational to assume their predictions to be nothing more than wasteful conjecture. Within the books of Luke and Matthew, the time line Jesus describes bares a glaring discordance.

"Truly I say to you, this generation will not pass away until all things take place. Heaven and earth will pass away, but My words will not pass away." - Luke 21:32-33

"And this gospel of the kingdom shall be preached in the whole world for a witness to all the nations, and then the end shall come." - Matthew 24:14

Jesus seems just as fallible as you or I. Why would he have said that the end will happen within that specific generation, while also insisting the end wouldn't come until the entire world has heard his message? If he truly did exist, and he made such errors as this, his status of perfection ought to be stricken away from him. The Bible also portrays the character Paul, who after a conversion became Jesus' "right hand man" to spread his word to those who have not heard it. Yet with such a title as Paul had, he and Jesus seemed to have found a way to disagree on the nature of the rapture Paul believed to be looming in the distance.

"After that, we who are still alive and are left will be caught up together with them in the clouds to meet the Lord in the air. And so we will be with the Lord forever." - 1 Thessalonians 4:17

"As it was in the days of Noah, so it will be at the coming of the Son of Man. For in the days before the flood, people were eating and drinking, marrying and giving in marriage, up to the day Noah entered the ark; and they knew nothing about what would happen until the flood came and took them all away. That is how it will be at the coming of the Son of Man. Two men will be in the field; one will be taken and the other left. Two women will be grinding with a hand mill; one will be taken and the other left." - Matthew 24:37-42

Paul clearly wrote in his letter that when Christ returns, all will be drawn to Heaven and from there they would be judged by God, while Jesus spoke of only his faithful followers being involved in the rapture. If you were to read a math text book that proposed both 2+2=3 and 2+2=5, which would you believe? You would find that perplexing, and wonder why they considered both ideas as true. If an honest and intelligent reader attempts to draw a conclusion from these texts, they would recognize the immaturity of the composer. This type of cherry-picking is quite common among Christians, using either or to support their chosen assertion. When those who claim that the end is upon us, they begin with their theory and find evidence to support that assumption, which is an inappropriate approach to answering a question. Their handling of the situation is just as flawed as the books upon which they've gathered their information.

Since man has begun attempting to prepare for the end of the world, predictions have been made when this will actually happen. There have been over 200 failed Christian predictions, most of which taken place within the past few hundred years. Recently, a gentleman proclaimed that on May 21, 2011, Jesus would return to rapture those who faithfully follow him. That event would precede the end of the natural or which was to take place 5 months later. To his amazement, the rapture had failed to occur as he predicted. He quickly explained that this must have been a "spiritual" rapture, and that the October 21 apocalypse would actually take place. We all know how that eventually turned out for him. Unfortunately, his actions lead to the suicide of a young Russian girl who, fearful of the imposing judgment, could not handle that emotional baggage that accommodated those claims. It is sad to see someone so recklessly solicit this fear inside the most fragile of individuals. He hasn't been the only one to find error in a prediction of this sort with harmful results.

The less mainstream Jehovah's Witnesses have become known for their fallacious end of time predictions. They, like most Christians, believe what is being preached at the pulpit. This blind faith coupled with a mandated adherence to their doctrine would eventually lead to much criticism within the confines of their own religion. After eight failed predictions, a reformation took place within the body of the church. They have also attempted to rectify these assumptions claiming that they are merely human, and from time to time can be found wrong. As a result, an enormous amount of followers donated their possessions and money in preparation for the end, which led to a large fallout in the number of members.

When someone takes on the responsibility of thousands of individual's hopes and wishes, no matter how ridiculous they may be, they ought to be held accountable. Their hasty assumptions can bring pain and suffering to those who believe it. These peddlers of false hope break a moral code that their beloved Jesus would even uphold. The same thing can be said of the Jehovah Witnesses. If they instruct their followers to sell their possessions and quit their jobs, they ought to be sure their predictions are true. Otherwise, their negligence to their member's well-being shows that their credibility as a valid religion is slim to none. The phrase "history repeats itself" can be said about these false predictions and as long as strife exists in this world, they will persist.

Too much energy has been spent worrying about an end-of-times event. These speculations have been based on a litany of ridiculous conjecture compounded with the erroneous text that Christians possess. The fact is that these faith-based claims wouldn't have been, or continue to be, made if Christianity hadn't interjected the very idea of an apocalyptic rapture. Christians ought to ask themselves why God, who is all powerful, must send them through a period of pain and suffering before he returns to save his believers. I find not a shred of reason behind God's methodology.

Once an individual can critically examine the text of which they derive their faith, they will have no other option but to disregard these absurd notions. Of course there are more detrimental events that could cause the end of civilization as we know it. As religious violence has increased, so has the ability to create substantially destructible weaponry. We've almost drained this world of its natural resources and caused irreversible damage to the ozone layer. The end of the world is no longer in the hands of a god as once believed, but now we've created the ability to kill ourselves.

Christianity gives an individual the idea that this world is theirs for the taking, because the rapture will save them from a naturalistic apocalypse. This irrational egocentrism will cause our end, not an invisible creator with a delirious way of going about saving those who love him. Instead of worrying about their own salvation and the return of God, Christians ought to focus on the real problems we face these days. Until then, I will worry about the future of our civilization and the integrity of this planet.

CHAPTER SIX
YOU'RE WHAT'S IMPORTANT

"The only position that leaves me with no cognitive dissonance is atheism. It is not a creed. Death is certain, replacing both the siren-song of Paradise and the dread of Hell. Life on this earth, with all its mystery and beauty and pain, is then to be lived far more intensely: we stumble and get up, we are sad, confident, insecure, feel loneliness and joy and love. There is nothing more; but I want nothing more." - Christopher Hitchens, The Portable Atheist

It was a cold January night. I remember sitting in my first Alcoholics Anonymous meeting a number of years ago feeling miserable, sick, and alone. The room was lively; snacks were passed around, coffee was drank, and laughs were shared. I sat alone, wishing my depression would allow me to have a normal conversation with another human being. I remember wishing I had a driver's license that would allow me to leave, but since I did not, I was stuck in-between a rock and a hard place.

I was 21 then. I heavily drank for much of the previous year. 2010 was nothing but a litany of heartache, academic failures, lost friendships, and social deprivation. Most would be quick to blame their dependency on alcohol, but it was my fault. I let a long-lasting relationship end, fought with people who cared for me, and skipped classes because I felt I was too ill from the drinking. These could have been prevented had I not let my life slip away; only because I cared more for my whiskey-soaked existence than the opportunities and loved ones around me. I realized this in January of 2011 and I thought I would bring an end to it.

Which that is why I found myself sitting in an AA meeting. I cannot tell you about much of the meeting itself, only because I truly don't remember. One thing, though, has stuck with me and will continue to till I pass. I watched as other members took turns, sharing their stories of depression, rage, and sobriety. Their stories differed greatly, but one central theme brought them together: They all thanked God for their sobriety. I'm not talking about a few or most of them, I mean all of them. I refrained from speaking, only because I was sober for 1 day and I knew I had no one to thank besides myself.

I continued with the program for 6 months, which was all I could stand. I witnessed people come and go, from all walks of life, from 16 years old to 75 years old, people who were happy and people who were absolutely miserable. However it was their internal struggle I could not bear to watch. I could see them attempt to deal with an unnerving dilemma: their chemical dependency versus why their God had yet to remove the addiction. Many times, members would stand and ask, "Why is it that my faith has yet to rid my body of this disease?" I walked away from the program. By this point I was well past drinking. I cannot tell you if I had a real dependency (though my first few sober days consisted of binge-eating, headaches, and anxiety) but I knew then that I was incapable of drinking responsibly, so my best bet was to abstain; which I'm proud to say that I've gone over 3 years without even a sip.

So that brings me to the point of this portion. One of the most ghastly implications of faith - predominantly Christianity - is that it persuades it's victims to believe in a plan; a plan predetermined by a divine commander. As part of that plan, this divine commander has great things lined up for the believer; never mind the bad things, remember he has no control over the bad things that happen. We see this so often that it almost goes unnoticed. Sometimes, however, I do. Whatever it may be, its credit is usually God. Whether it's a loss in waist-size, a hasty recovery, an excellent test score, or a job promotion, God somehow had something to do with these instances. If this were part of a divine plan, surely human abilities would have no effect on it, right?

If those positive instances were predestined by God, I press anyone to not exercise, refrain from doctors' visits, don't study for an upcoming exam, or skip work periodically and expect those results. Usually the results of those that I've named will prove negative. Why is that? Certainly God has some great things in line, right?

Those of faith always have an answer for why bad things happen, why their god seems to have no control over the bad things, and why the good things are wonderful blessings. I believe these to be nothing more than excuses and empty defenses pedaled from a delusion; a delusion that influences those of faith to understand nothing while claiming knowledge of the unknowable.

It's sad to see so many give thanks where the credit isn't due. I want everyone to understand their capabilities; capabilities available even considering the nonexistence of God. Good things (and bad things) happen to atheists whom hold no belief in the god many worship. Success and good fortune is in our hands and the hands of other human beings. We need to set aside this childish behavior. If your hard work has paid off, thank yourself. If your surgery was successful, thank your doctor. Does a God who's only concerned with blessings and not misfortunes deserve any credit what so ever? I don't think so. This "God of Good Fortune" most tend to worship is the least-deserving of any postulated god found throughout history. You're life - your successes and your setbacks - is in your hands. Don't wait for a miracle. Go out and get it done. When something good does happen, be humble. When something bad happens, don't give up.

It's that simple.

CHAPTER SEVEN
A CLOSING STATEMENT FOR THE CHRISTIAN

To determine the actual existence of something, we need to define truth. I'm not speaking of the truth as it pertains to personal preference, but in the context of something that can yield sufficient evidence to prove its being. You or I could take a handful of sand and feel the grains pour between our fingers, and with that we can conclude sand is an element of reality. When it comes to the absolute truth of a metaphysical being, the elements of reality lay only in the consciousness of the beholder. Claims of the supernatural that exist within the doctrine of Christianity directly oppose all of what reality has been proven to be. Many have attempted to justify that irrationality by seeking answers where science has shined its everlasting eye.

Often, you have been abruptly met with a preponderance of evidence proving that your understanding of truth may have been altered by your theistic beliefs. Still, the emotion that is derived from such beliefs is what binds your essence to such a detrimental notion. Is it a mystery why Muslim and Jewish individuals feel the same emotion when "in the presence of God", but all have a different theistic outlook? This is because that specific emotional comfort is a creation of your mind in response to a belief that has been hammered into place since you could conceive thought. Once the origin of such emotions is recognized, reality will become much clearer. God has never been a viable answer how this world was created, why we are here, what purpose we serve, and what happens after death. He has only been used as a subconscious alternative to the fear that absolute truth may present.

Those answers you seek may be unobtainable by science as of today, and Christianity can provide that internal comfort that is so sought after. Remember though, they are only self-satisfying, and when it becomes that type of element within your internal consciousness, it exits from the confines of truth. Once you finally accept that fact, a free intelligence and the clarity of reality is yours to be had. God certainly needs to go, so that which a much more fruitful life can be enjoyed.

ABOUT THE AUTHOR

J. D. Brucker was born near Chicago, Illinois. He is an atheist author and blogger, a secular humanist, and an outspoken anti-theist. He studied world history at Eastern Illinois University. Brucker believes that non-theism, skepticism, humanism, and secularism are our greatest allies. Currently, Brucker writes for the *Atheist Republic* and *Patheos* websites. Other works can be found on various secular websites, including *The Richard Dawkins Foundation for Reason and Science* and *The Natural Skeptic*. His first book (*Improbable: Is There Any Reason To Believe In God?*) was published in December of 2013 by Dangerous Little Books. It was then re-released as a self-published work under the title *Improbable: Issues with the God Hypothesis* in November of 2014. In February of 2015, Atheist Republic released his second book *God Needs To Go: Why Christian Beliefs Fail*.

You can visit his website at: www.jdbrucker.com

Follow him on Twitter at: @jdbrucker

16353707R00055

Printed in Great Britain
by Amazon